Begin to write

Beginning to write is lots of fun — nursery characters show how it's done.

Follow the trails from left to right – first with your finger, then with your pencil.

Encourage your child to work from left to right, as that is the way writing goes. Tracing the lines with her finger first will help make the writing easier. Why not sing the rhymes together as she works?

Incy Wincy Spider

Incy Wincy Spider,
Climbed up the spout;
Down came the rain
And washed the spider out.

Draw lines showing Incy going up and down the spout, and draw more rain coming down.

*Out came the sunshine,
And dried up all the rain;
Incy Wincy Spider
Climbed the spout again.*

Draw round the sun and the puddles.

Talk to your child about the different types of lines. Which are curved? Which are straight? Curved lines will be easier for your child to make than straight ones.

Little Bo Peep

Little Bo Peep has lost her sheep. Mend her fences or she'll weep and weep.

Now draw round her faithful sheep and give them long straight grass to eat.

Encourage your child to make continuous, flowing movements with her pencil.

Three little pigs

Little Pig is in a fix. Build his house with long straight sticks.

Now the sticks are on the ground!

Climb the ladder and try again. Perhaps this straw will make a den.

Oh dear, we're on the run again!

Talk to your child about the story of The three little pigs. *What do the pigs use to build a house with next?*

Safe and sound

Draw lines to make tiles and bricks. Then colour them so they'll be fixed.

Grumpy Wolf is off again. Follow his trail to another tale.

Mazes and trails will help your child to develop hand-eye coordination, concentration and pencil control.

Little Red Riding Hood

Follow Little Red Riding Hood's trail through the wood. Will she get to Grandma's house?

Who rescues Grandma?

The grumpy wolf has gone away. Now Little Red Riding Hood is free to play.

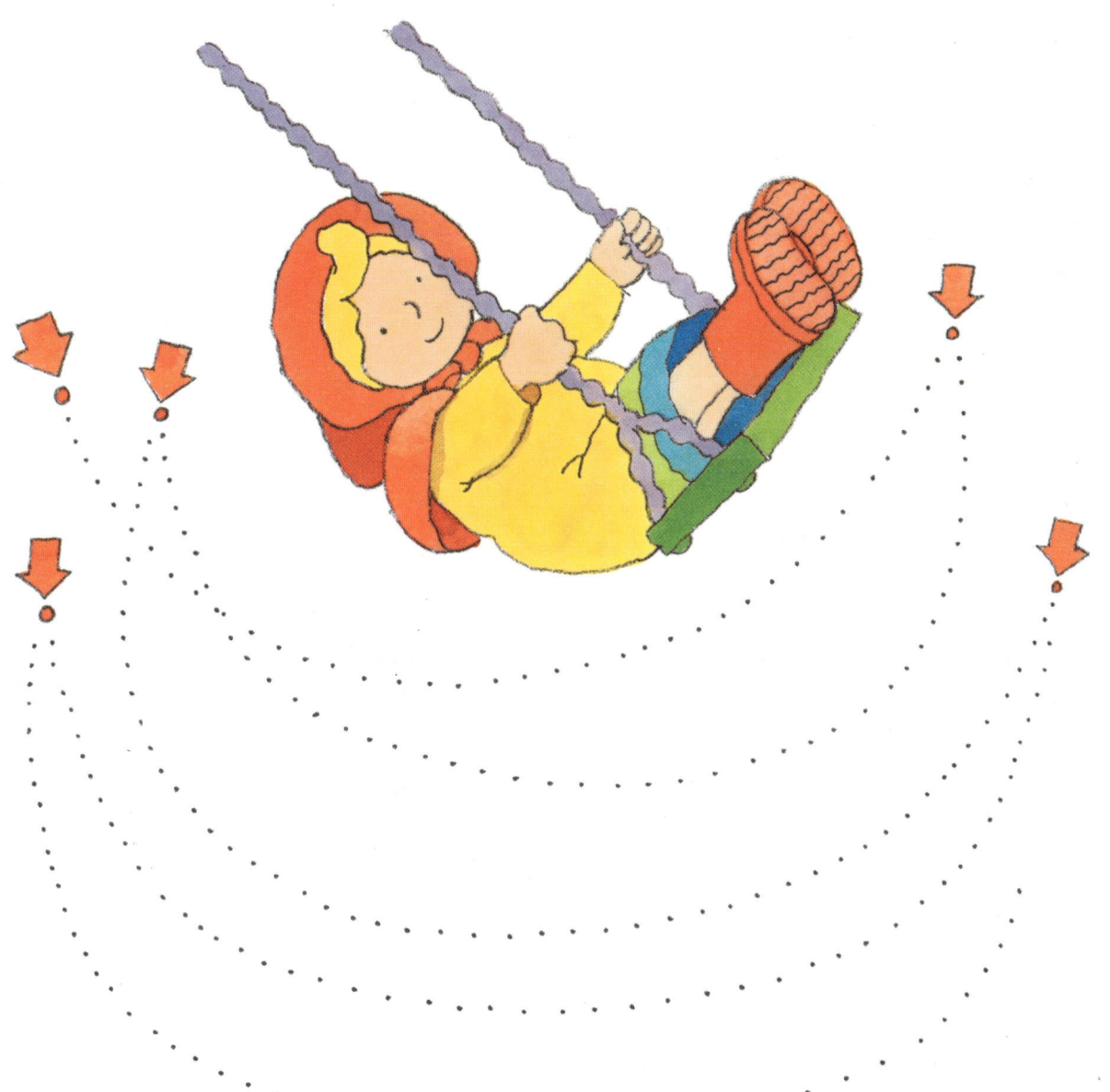

As she swings high and low, move your pencil to and fro!

Your child will enjoy making free backwards and forwards swinging movements like these. Let her do as many as she likes!

Jack be nimble

Join in Jack's jumping game.

Jack be nimble, Jack be quick.

Jack jump over the candlestick.

(…and now go round it!)

Sally's dancing in bright pink boots.
March your pencil along each route.

Sally go round the sun,
Sally go round the moon,

Sally go round the chimney pots
On a Saturday afternoon.

Lots of letters involve making circles in an anti-clockwise direction. This can be tricky at first so don't worry if your child strays a little from the lines. You could also practise making circles in the air using big, bold arm movements, then smaller finger movements.

The Grand Old Duke of York

The Grand Old Duke of York's soldiers march in a line.

Up and down the hills they go, sometimes high, sometimes low.

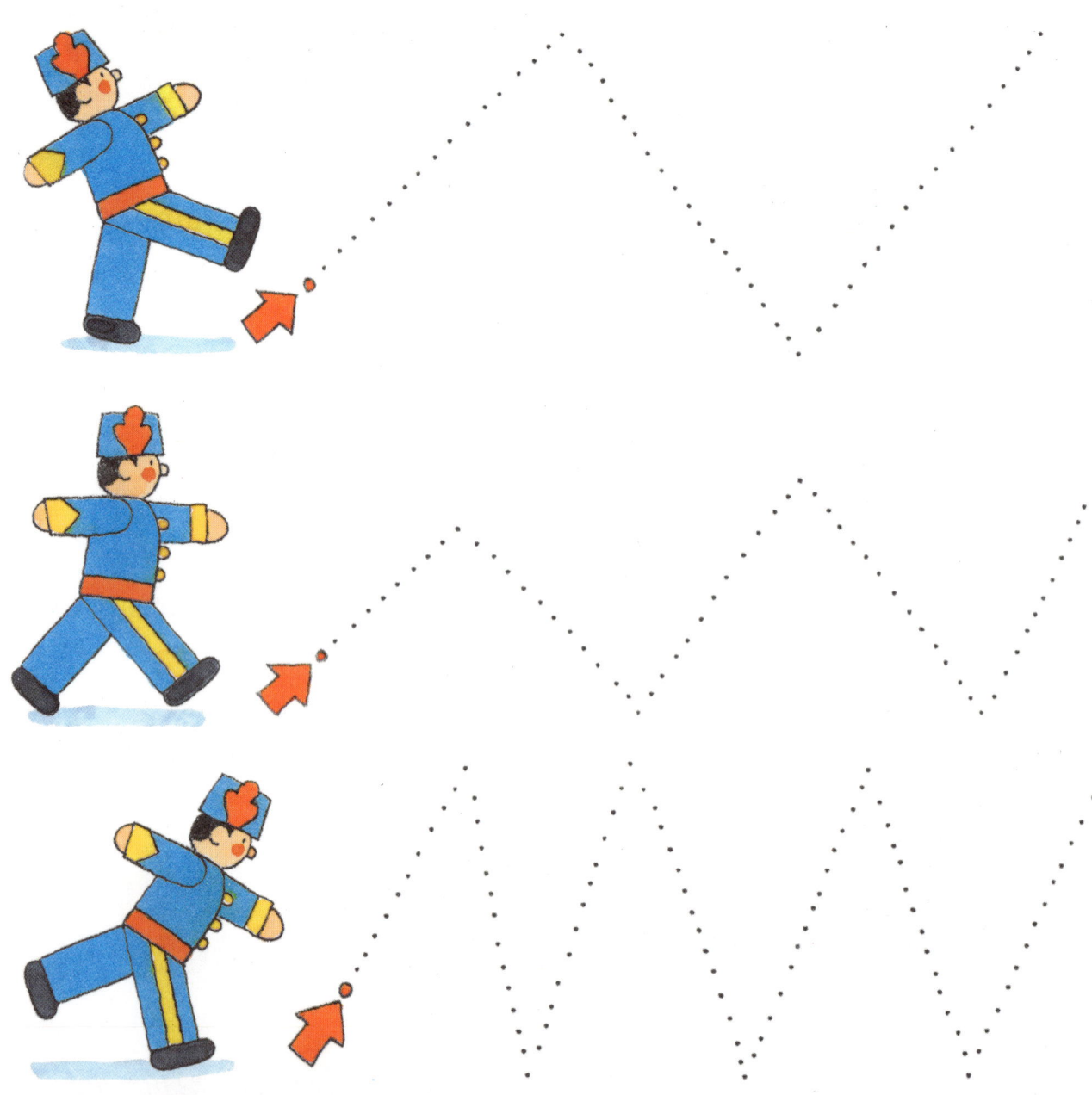

Can you follow where the soldiers march with your pencil?

Draw a fort for the Grand Old Duke of York. Then colour it.

Encourage your child to add more details to the picture, for example, a door and windows or decorations on the flag. Adding her own details will help her to feel more confident about making marks on a page.

The wheels on the bus

Draw on the wheels and make them round as the bus speeds along the ground.

The wheels on the bus go…

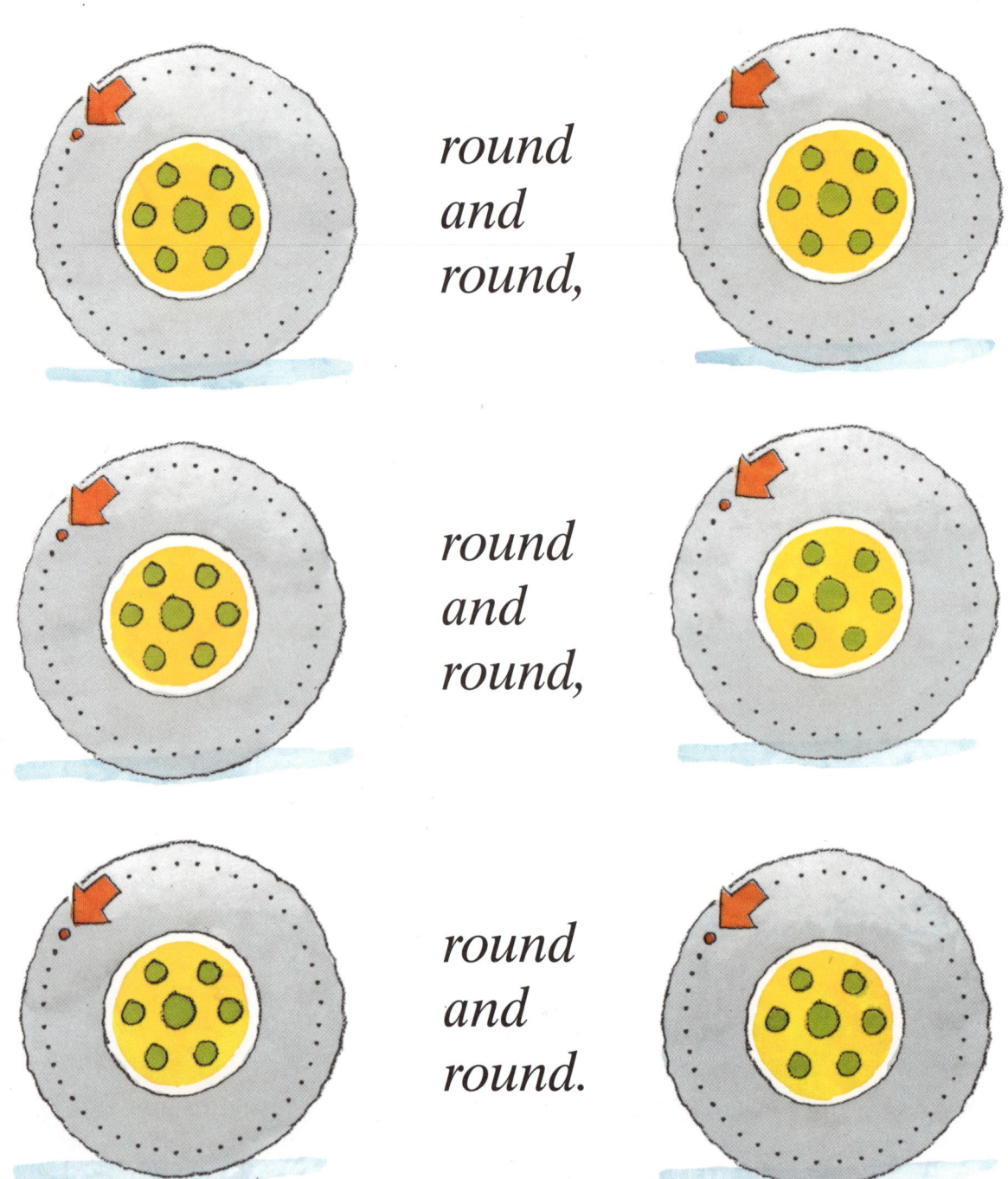

round and round,

round and round,

round and round.

*The wheels on the bus go round and round...
all day long!*

The wheels on a bike also go round and round. Draw along the dotted lines.

Circles are tricky for a young child to draw, so give her lots of practice and fun. Sing the song together as she draws the wheels on the bus.

Jack and Jill

Jack and Jill went up the hill
To fetch a pail of water.

Draw the lines on Jack and Jill's clothes and colour the picture.

When Jack fell down, he dropped his pail! Can you draw the water spilling out?

Drawing these varied patterns will help your child when she comes to form letters.

Hey, diddle, diddle

Draw on the lines and finish the picture.

Hey, diddle, diddle,
The cat and the fiddle,
The cow jumped over the moon.
The little dog laughed
To see such sport,
And the dish ran away
With the spoon!

Who is running away with the spoon?

Say the rhyme to your child and look for details together in the picture. Ask for example: 'Who is jumping over the moon?'

Teddy bear's show

Before you finish the book and go,
Teddy wants to put on a show.

Teddy bear, teddy bear, stand up straight.

Teddy bear, teddy bear, juggle with plates.

Teddy bear, teddy bear, climb the stairs.
Teddy bear, teddy bear, say your prayers.

Finish the stairs and the bed so that Teddy can go to sleep!

When your child has finished the page, congratulate her on her hard work and success. You could make her an 'I've started writing' badge or poster.

Yum! Yum!

I spy with my little eye a pie for:

Ask someone to help you write your name on the pie.

Write your child's name lightly on the pie and help her to trace over the letters.